WORDS
OF
COMFORT

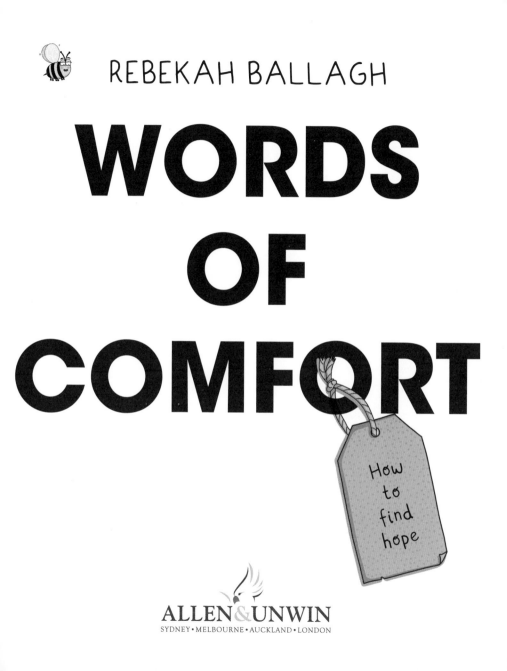

REBEKAH BALLAGH

WORDS OF COMFORT

How to find hope

ALLEN&UNWIN
SYDNEY • MELBOURNE • AUCKLAND • LONDON

CONTENTS

Welcome, I'm so glad you're here

Grief comes in all shapes and sizes, and in many different forms. You may have picked up this book because:

- you have lost a loved one
- you are experiencing a separation/relationship break-up
- you have had a major change in your life
- you are battling through health issues
- you have a friend or loved one who is grieving
- you work with people experiencing grief

Whatever your reason, you are in the right place.

Grief is a very intense experience, and can be very hard to put into words. It is fraught with conflicting and complicated emotions and can leave you feeling helpless, hopeless, overwhelmed and unsure of what to do and where to turn.

Words of Comfort is here to help.

This book is your companion in grief. A guiding light, an empathetic safe space, a beacon of hope and a place where you can come to sit with your grief. The pages ahead are divided into three parts.

Chapter One explores the experience of grieving, and the emotions and the thoughts that may surface during this difficult process. Chapter Two opens up a toolbox of strategies and words of comfort to help you navigate through your grief. And Chapter Three takes a look at some of the things we can learn from grief. The silver linings . . . and the ways you may just grow from the experience.

Some of the words and illustrations ahead may be just what you are after, and some may not be the right fit for the form of grief you are experiencing right now. Take what you need and leave what you don't.

I sincerely hope you find some comfort in these pages. Know that you are not alone in your experience of grief. Whatever you may be thinking and feeling right now, trust that it is normal, it is allowed, it is all part of the process.

— Rebekah Ballagh

Chapter One
GOING THROUGH IT

This chapter aims to hold up a mirror to some of the experiences you may have while grieving. Hopefully you feel seen in these pages, identifying with the words and images ahead, and connecting with the knowledge that your journey through grief is normal. Some of the pages may resonate perfectly with what you are going through, while others may not feel like quite the right fit.

Everyone will experience grief in different ways. This can be influenced by so many things: who you are, how you manage emotions, your previous life experiences, the family narratives you were brought up with, the form of grief you are going through, how you interpret the 'severity' of your loss, whether your grief felt like a sudden loss or a gradual change, or whether there is shock or trauma present for you.

Pick and choose the pages ahead that you connect with the most, and 'put aside' the ones that don't resonate with you right now.

SOME REASONS PEOPLE GRIEVE

relationship ending

death of a pet

death of a loved one

family member's illness

personal injury/ illness

loss of a dream/goal

job loss

job change

life change after baby

abortion

miscarriage/ stillbirth

losing a friend

'failing' at something

change in schools

moving house/city

a poor relationship with a family member

child leaving home

losing your business/ financial loss

Sometimes you may find yourself juggling
multiple forms of grief at once . . .

GRIEF...

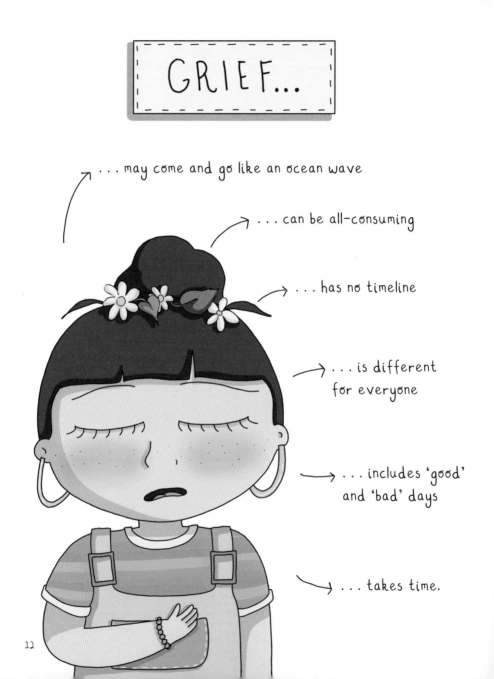

... may come and go like an ocean wave

... can be all-consuming

... has no timeline

... is different for everyone

... includes 'good' and 'bad' days

... takes time.

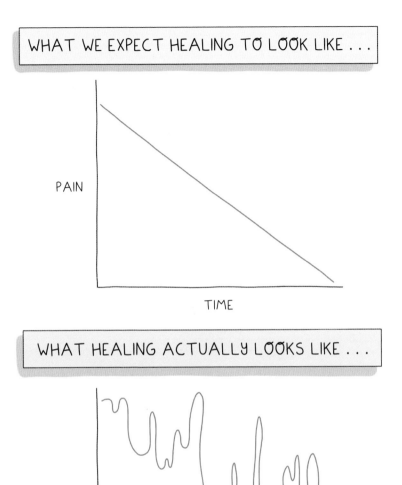

WHAT WE EXPECT HEALING TO LOOK LIKE . . .

PAIN

TIME

WHAT HEALING ACTUALLY LOOKS LIKE . . .

PAIN

TIME

Grief may come in ebbs
and flows like the ocean
. . . calm at times . . .

A sense of panic, fear or anxiety. Feeling trapped, out of control or homesick.

Deep sadness, depression, guilt, loneliness or sorrow. Feeling overwhelmed, crushed, exhausted or drained. Feeling alone, with a deep longing.

Feeling physically sick, in pain, dizzy or headachey. Experiencing an aching or heavy heart and chest.

Feeling empty, numb, on autopilot, lost or in a daze. A sense of disconnection from reality.

Feeling okay, forgetting about it for a bit, feeling happiness or joy, enjoying memories or laughing.

Feeling shocked, traumatised, jumpy, anxious, worried or on edge.

Feeling angry, rageful or irritable.

GRIEF MIGHT FEEL LIKE...

headache

tiredness/ exhaustion

dizzy/ lightheaded

foggy brain/ thoughts

difficulty breathing

urge to cry/wail

aching feeling in your heart

tight chest/ chest pain

rapid heartbeat

butterflies/ stomach dropping

loss of appetite

feeling numb

nausea

body aches

physical pain

shaking

dissociated/ disconnected

waves of pain/ rushes of nerves

Sometimes you may feel all
alone and lost at sea.

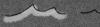 

Change can be exciting and
scary at the same time.

Change can leave you with a knot
of stress in your tummy.

You might feel like you want
to bottle it all up.

parasympathetic
nervous system

sympathetic
nervous system

The parasympathetic and sympathetic nervous systems make up the two branches of your automatic nervous system.

When the parasympathetic nervous system is activated, it turns on our 'rest and digest' response.

When the sympathetic nervous system is activated, it turns on our threat response.

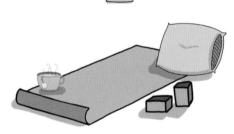

'CALM'

'ALARM'

Loss sometimes feels like
a vast homesickness with
no home to return to.

It's true that you can
be homesick for a time
rather than a place.

You may have lots of 'why' questions . . .

. . . that don't seem to have any answers.

It's normal to feel irritable when
experiencing loss and change.

A loss can make you feel like everything has just stopped and you don't know how to carry on.

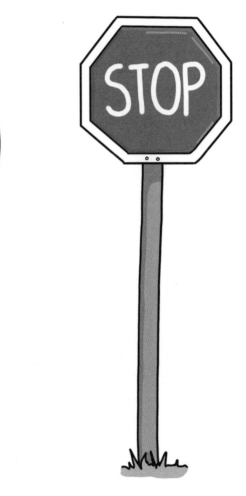

The feeling of loss can be quite unexplainable.

When you lose someone you love, the grief and loss are as deep as the love and joy they gave you.

Events, milestones or
unexpected reminders may
trigger a wave of grief -
often in the most
unanticipated moments.

NORMAL THINGS TO DO
WHEN GRIEVING . . .

stay in bed all day

dwell

carry on like nothing happened

ruminate

have trouble sleeping

feel afraid to be alone

stop doing things you enjoy

avoid people

pretend you are okay

distract yourself

still talk to them

visit places that remind you

look at old pictures

lose your appetite

not know what to do with yourself

vent to people

cry - a little, a lot, at random . . . or not cry at all

sit and stare at the wall

smell their things

get annoyed at people

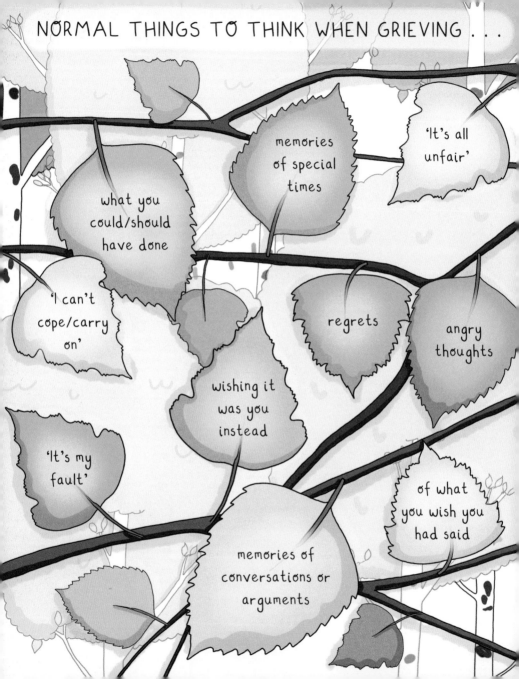

THINGS you may DISCOVER while GRIEVING...

 Closure is an abstract concept and has no place in grieving. Try to let go of the idea you need to 'shut the door' on your grief.

 Over time you will integrate the loss; not 'get over it' or 'let it go'. This doesn't mean the immense pain continues forever, it means you learn to redirect your love and connection after the loss.

 Grief doesn't follow neat stages. It's messy. It's hard, and it's confusing.

Grief can make people uncomfortable and sometimes you will have awkward moments with those around you.

 People might say silly things that hurt you by accident.

 Grief can be a transformative and healing process.

Grief might make you question your faith.

You might feel like you're going crazy.

 It's normal to feel guilt.

 Anger is a normal part of grief.

 Grief might make you re-evaluate your life, your values and your goals. You might make changes and reprioritise, and that's okay.

 You might need to replay the loss or change, and debrief things a lot. Your brain is trying to process it all.

 Grief can make you feel resentment towards other people and the size of their 'problems'. It's okay to feel that way for a while.

 Time does not heal all wounds. Some wounds you learn to live with.

 It's okay to hold strong boundaries. You don't have to justify them. You can tell people when they aren't being helpful.

You can express your emotions in whatever way works for you; not how other people think you should.

Blame and regret are normal experiences. Go easy on yourself and lean into compassion.

You may notice a pain, an aching
or a weight in your chest.

Many people experience a sense of guilt with grief . . .

Loss can leave you feeling shocked.

It can sometimes feel like the people around you are avoiding you or like they don't care while you grieve. In reality, they may feel uncomfortable, overwhelmed, sad, triggered or at a loss for words of comfort.

They still care.

Grief can be frightening and make you
feel like you want to shut it out.

You may notice your brain feels
foggy, or you feel confused
or a little spaced out.

It's normal to feel numb, tired,
weak or confused when experiencing loss.

Anger is normal,
anger is okay;
allow anger to be.

You may experience panic attacks or immense anxiety while grieving.

Chapter Two
GETTING THROUGH IT

The pages ahead aim to bring you a sense of having a 'life raft' to cling to. Grief can leave us feeling like we are lost at sea, being churned up by waves with nothing to hold on to for stability.

This chapter explores words of comfort and important reminders to help guide you on your way, as well as tools and strategies that may help support you in your loss.

There is no quick fix for grief. At times you might feel desperate to be rid of feeling this way; however, we cannot just turn off emotions. But while it's true that there is no instant 'cure' for grief, there are certainly tonics that help to ease the pain or support the journey. I hope you find some of that comfort in the following pages.

Instead of trying to 'let go',
'get over it' or 'move on' . . .

perhaps we should focus on learning to live with
the grief, alongside it - learning to live our
life with the loss still in our heart.

There is no 'right way' to grieve.
There is no roadmap for navigating loss.

Aim to process,
not suppress,
your emotions

THE KEY TO PROCESSING

ACKNOWLEDGE

Acknowledge the emotion:
'Oh hello, grief'
'I'm noticing sadness'

LINK

Link the trigger:
'It makes sense that I feel this way
given what I have lost/been through'

ALLOW

Allow the emotion to be and to pass:
'It's okay that you are here'

We grieve far more than just the physical absence that loss brings. We grieve the intangible . . . the loss of a shared life, future dreams, the loss of little things . . . the inside jokes, the security, the mundane, the routine, the things that you thought annoyed you but that now you would give anything to have again. We miss the comfort, the familiarity, the abstract . . .

How to ASK FOR HELP when you need it

* Remember, you are not a burden. People like to help, it makes them feel useful.

* Text, call or email family and friends. Say: 'I'm struggling right now, are you able to help with . . .'

* Be prepared that some people may be 'tapped out' too, and unable to help. That doesn't mean they don't care or your needs aren't valid. Reach out to someone else.

* Try support groups, counselling, therapy or support lines.

* It's okay to ask for help even when you don't know what you need. You can say 'I'm feeling really low right now. I don't know what I need but I don't want to be alone.'

* You might not want to 'talk about it' – that's okay! You can say 'Can we do something distracting to take my mind off things for a bit?'

* If you don't have many people close to you, you can still reach out to someone you trust: 'I know we don't talk much, but I'm going through a tough time and I'd love to chat if you are free?'

* Remember, it's okay to be vulnerable. Asking for help is not weak.

* Remember that people can't read your mind. Sometimes you have to ask for exactly what you need.

* Know that you are deserving of love, support, help and care.

LIFE GROWS AROUND GRIEF...

At first the loss is consuming and takes up a lot of your life . . .

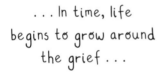

. . . In time, life begins to grow around the grief . . .

. . . The loss doesn't shrink but it becomes less dominant . . .

. . . Soon, life is full again. The grief will always remain and be something that you carry with you, but your world will grow more colourful around the loss.

When you are going through a tough time you may find it difficult to sleep. Here are some tips to help you get a good night's rest.

☾ Try a relaxing 'wind-down' routine 30 minutes before bed - e.g. chamomile tea, a bath and some gratitude journalling.

☾ Go to bed and get up at roughly the same time each day.

☾ Use your bed only for sleep - i.e. not for work/movies, etc. (It helps your brain form the association that bed = sleep.)

☾ Exercise early, rather than late, in the day.

☾ No screen time for half an hour prior to bed.

☾ No caffeine from late afternoon onwards.

☾ Try diffusing some lavender oil each night before bed.

...raw and painful to start, it consumes your attention...

...then tender but less dominating of your life ...

...then over time the wound begins to naturally heal.

HEALING CAN GET COMPLICATED...

Sometimes if we don't tend to the wound it doesn't heal.

If this happens we can reach out for extra help and support.

Sometimes the wound leaves a scar that we learn to live with.

CREATE A MEMORY BOX

Fill the box with things that remind you of the special
person, place, pet or thing that you are grieving.
When you need time to pause and reminisce, you can
sit and look through the memory box.

Memory Box

DEALING WITH GUILT

Sometimes during grief we experience feelings of guilt. If you notice this, treat yourself as you would a loved one . . . What would you say to reassure and comfort them? How can you be gentle with yourself and show compassion?

Poses to support turning inward, reflection, calming and protecting the heart

You might like to place a blanket over your heart to create a feeling of protection.

Corpse pose (savasana)

Child's pose (bālāsana)

Legs up the wall (viparita karani)

Poses to support heart opening to bring emotions to the surface for processing

Sphinx pose
(salamba bhujangasana)

Camel pose
(ustrasana)

Bridge pose
(setu bandha sarvāngāsana)

FEELING A LUMP IN YOUR THROAT?

This sensation is normal with grief.

It can also be a message to you about holding back tears and emotion. Check in and ask youself:

☐ Do I need to have a good cry?

☐ Does my body feel like wailing or shouting?

☐ Am I suppressing something?

☐ Do I need to scream into a pillow?

☐ Do I need to talk to someone?

MANTRAS

Take a comfy seat,
inhale deeply and repeat
these mantras . . .

- I am capable of getting
  through hard times.

- I focus on things within
  my control.

- I allow my feelings to 'just be'.

- I take it one day at a time.

- I look for comfort in the
  little things.

- I lean into my emotions.

Things to help lift you up . . .

It's normal to feel like
you can't let go.

It's okay to laugh and be happy
when you're grieving . . .

Laughter can be a relief as it releases
positive hormones.

Allow yourself to have fun - it isn't disloyal.

You can also:

- tell funny stories about the person/thing/time you are
  grieving

- remember funny moments

- distract yourself with funny movies/books/TV.

Trying to contain grief is like
trying to put a tornado in a jar.

Treat grief like a visitor . . .

Acknowledge it when it pops in.

Welcome it and allow it to be there.

Listen to what it needs.

Sit with it.

Know it will not always be there.

See it off when it's time for it to leave.

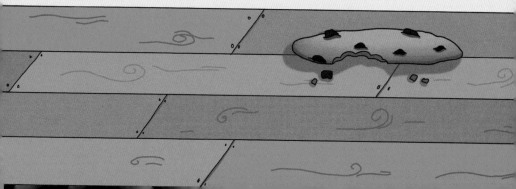

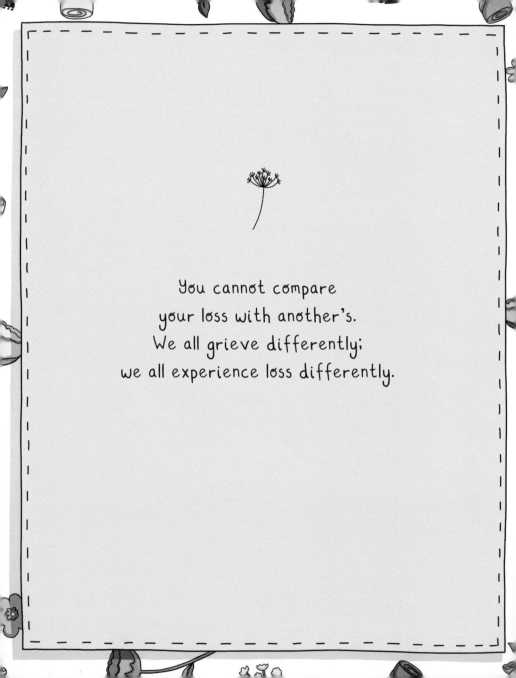

You cannot compare
your loss with another's.
We all grieve differently;
we all experience loss differently.

Sometimes, the very best
medicine is a good cry.

SAFE-PLACE VISUALISATION

It's time to create a | space | in your mind
that you can return to whenever you need
to 'escape' and feel safe...

Step 1: Close your eyes and bring a place to mind that makes you feel safe, grounded, protected and content. It may be somewhere you have been before or it could be a place you create in your imagination. You might picture a warm sandy beach, a sheltered forest, a fragrant meadow or a quiet chair by a fire in a library – it's up to you.

Step 2: Imagine as many details as you can – the smells, the sounds, the way it feels, the little details.

Step 3: Breathe deeply and imagine exploring this place, discovering more and more.

Step 4: Return here whenever you like, just by closing your eyes.

Get outside when you can.
Move your body when
you can.

Do it, even if you
don't feel like it.

Movement and nature
are healing.

Allow this feeling to be here.

Give yourself permission to feel whatever is present right now, and grant that emotion space.

Trust that it won't always be this intense or consuming.

Light a candle and sit with it as it burns.
Create a space to honour the memory
and the emotion.

Talk.
Talk about it.
Share memories.
Laugh at the stories.
Talk to a therapist.
Remember the good times.
Discuss the bad.
Take up space with your words.
Name your emotions.
Speak to the person, the place,
the time, the thing that is gone.
Just keep talking.

All your feelings are
rational and valid.

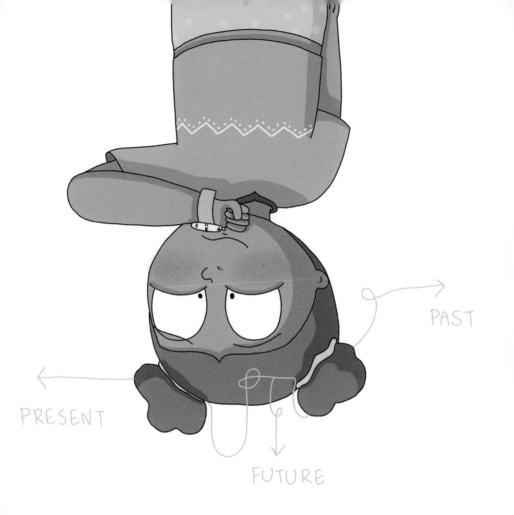

Time can become a topsy-turvy, strange and
tricky concept when you are grieving.

It may help to take one moment, one hour,
one day or one task at a time.

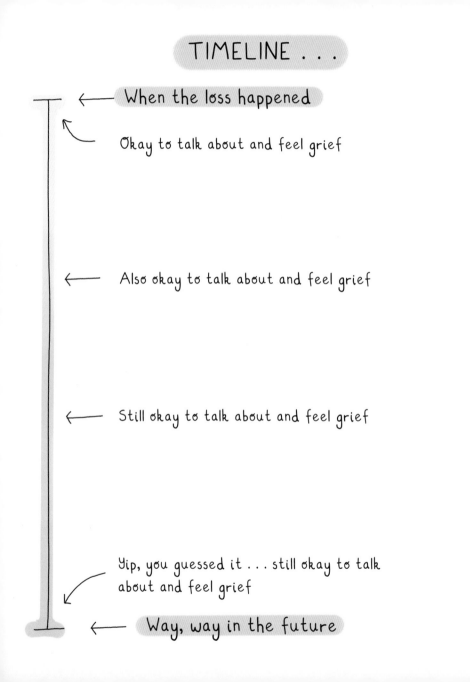

GROUNDING EXERCISE

This tool is a great way to become present, and is especially useful when you feel overwhelmed by your thoughts or emotions. Simply take a few deep breaths and notice . . .

5 things you can see

4 things you can hear

3 things you can feel

2 things you can smell

1 thing you can taste

Check in and notice how you feel now . . .

'MUSIC THERAPY' FOR GRIEF

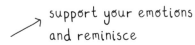

You can use music to . . .

→ support your emotions and reminisce

→ 'tap into' and release your emotions

↘ change or distract yourself from your emotions.

Play sad/slow music to 'lean into' feelings of grief or to allow yourself to have a good cry.

Play happy/upbeat music to give yourself a break, feel distracted or gently shift your mood.

There are times for acceptance . . .

. . . and there are times for distraction.

Externalise the feeling of loss . . .

Ask it what it needs from you and how you can best honour and care for yourself while this feeling is present.

During hard times, remind yourself
that life is a journey . . .

. . . where there are downs, there will also be ups again.

MINDFUL TEA-DRINKING EXERCISE

Take a mindful break with this calming and comforting sensory activity.
Make yourself a cuppa, sit somewhere cosy and . . .

Notice the colour of the tea and the steam rising from the cup . . . Look around you and notice the little details in the room before returning your attention to your mug.

Close your eyes and notice any sounds around you.

With your eyes still closed, take a long, slow inhale of your hot cuppa - savour the aroma.

Notice what you can feel . . . perhaps your back against the sofa, your feet on the floor and the warmth of the mug in your hands.

Lastly, take a sip of your tea and savour the tastes you are experiencing.

'THE BURRITO WRAP'

sensory calming

Many people find a sense of pressure very calming. This feeling of 'deep pressure' is called proprioceptive input; it relates to pressure on the body that can help to regulate your nervous system and soothe distress.

How to: grab a fluffy or weighted blanket and wrap yourself up tight.

This feeling of being snug and connected will calm you in minutes or even seconds.

Grief and guilt

You may feel a sense of guilt with grief . . .
guilt over what you did or didn't do,
guilt over what you did or didn't say
- this is normal.

It's a very painful feeling as you may not
be able to change anything.

So, what can you do?

- Journal about your feelings.

- Be compassionate and gentle with yourself.

- Remind yourself it was not your fault.

- Remind yourself that no one can predict the future or change things that are out of their control.

- Turn painful lessons into wisdoms.

- Practise gratitude.

- Challenge unhelpful thoughts with compassion and logic.

Shower compassion practice

This is a lovely gentle exercise to bring some kindness and gratitude into your day.

When you have a shower, think about and list . . .

- something you are grateful for to each part of your body

- three things in your life you are thankful for

- something you are holding on to or 'stuck' on, and three compassionate statements you can make to yourself to release and let go of these things.

HOT CHOCOLATE BREATH

Breathing techniques to soothe your mind . . .

Imagine you are holding a hot cuppa - slowly inhale as if taking in the aroma, then exhale through pursed lips as you visualise cooling the drink down.

Inhale for the count of 4, pause for the count of 4, exhale for the count of 4, pause for the count of 4, repeat.

SQUARE BREATH

1 2 3 4
INHALE

4
3 PAUSE
2
1

1
2 PAUSE
3
4

4 3 2 1
EXHALE

BELLY BREATH

Place your hands on your belly and observe as they rise and fall with each breath in and out.

Light a candle and direct each exhalation to gently flicker the flame without extinguishing it . . .

CANDLE BREATH

. . . and activate your parasympathetic nervous system to help regulate the stress response triggered by grief.

Try not to avoid your grief.
Suppressed emotions can pop up
in unexpected ways.

JOURNAL PROMPTS FOR GRIEF

- I can honour my grief by . . .

- I am grateful for . . .

- If my grief could talk, it would tell me . . .

- I can be more self-compassionate by . . .

- A comforting memory is . . .

- When I feel overwhelmed I can . . .

- What emotions are challenging for me to confront?
  How does this impact my grieving journey?

- Do I feel as if I have any roadblocks to grieving?

AFFIRMATIONS FOR
TIMES OF STRUGGLE

I was doing the best I could at
the time with what I knew.

I extend love and compassion
to my past self.

I was worthy of love then;
I am worthy of love now.

It is okay to struggle.

I send my past self thoughts
of healing and acceptance.

I allow myself grace, compassion
and kindness.

WORDS of COMFORT when Someone is GRIEVING

* 'I am so sorry you are going through this.'

* Share a memory.

* 'I don't have the right words right now, but I am here for you whenever you need.'

* 'I'm here to hold space for you, and to talk about it/them as much as you need.'

* 'It's okay to feel whatever you are feeling. It's all normal.'

* 'You didn't deserve this.'

* 'This must be so incredibly hard for you.'

* 'You can talk about it whenever you want.'

* 'It's okay to have both good and bad days.'

* Offer specific help: 'I have some meals cooked, what time suits to drop them off?' Or 'I'm free Tuesday and Sunday afternoons, what time works for you for me to come and do some housework?'

* Offer a hug, or just sit with them.

Allow your emotions and thoughts to flow freely, without judgement or attachment . . . like leaves floating downstream or clouds passing by overhead.

Trust your
inner strength.
You have the
resources you
need within you.

Chapter Three
BEEN THROUGH IT

Grief can feel utterly senseless and unfair. There is often not a reason why things happen. Grief is an unavoidable part of life, and a painful part ... But while nothing may feel like it explains or justifies why we go through such an experience, the following pages hope to bring some little rays of sunshine and silver linings.

Sometimes, while grief itself may feel unbearable and unfair, there are things we learn about the world, our lives and ourselves as a by-product of the grieving journey.

We may not be able to choose what happens to us, but we can choose what meaning we make of what happens and how we respond. It is up to us to honour our grief while simultaneously not being consumed by suffering.

The pure, unavoidable, attention-demanding, space-consuming rawness of grief may force us to learn that all emotions must be allowed space, and that the only way to deal with and process our feelings is to grant them our permission to just 'be'.

It's okay
to struggle.

You are stronger than you think.

All feelings
are valid.

All feelings
are allowed.

Your spirit was not made
to be contained. You were
designed to dance among
the stars and take up all
the space you need.

Sometimes grief shows you what really matters . . .

...it highlights the important stuff.

In grief we can find gratitude.

Through loss you may just learn that it's okay
to express yourself. It's okay to feel.

It's okay to go on living, to have a life
that carries on in a future you hadn't
imagined. It's okay to laugh again.
And it's always okay to cry again.

THERE ARE THINGS YOU CAN CONTROL IN LIFE & THERE ARE THINGS YOU CANNOT

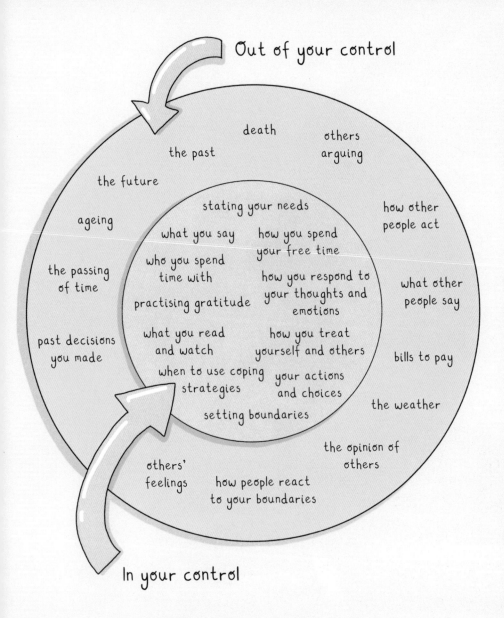

You will begin to slowly find joy in the little things again . . . to focus on small, glimmering moments in the present and to find wonder in the mundane.

We cannot change the past; we can only change the way we look at it.

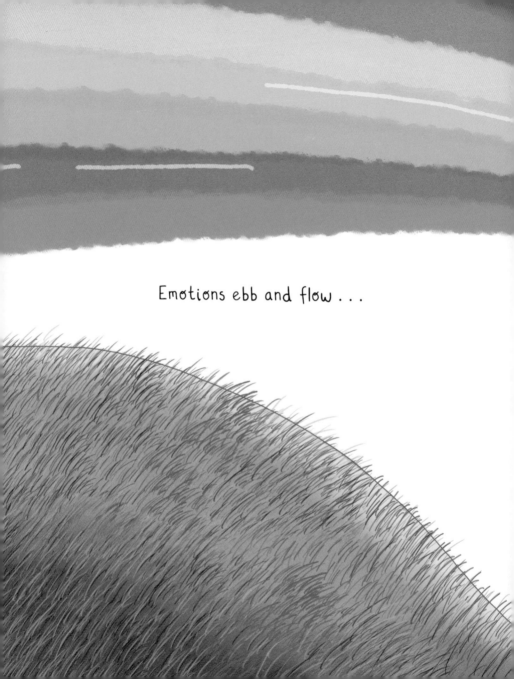

Emotions ebb and flow . . .

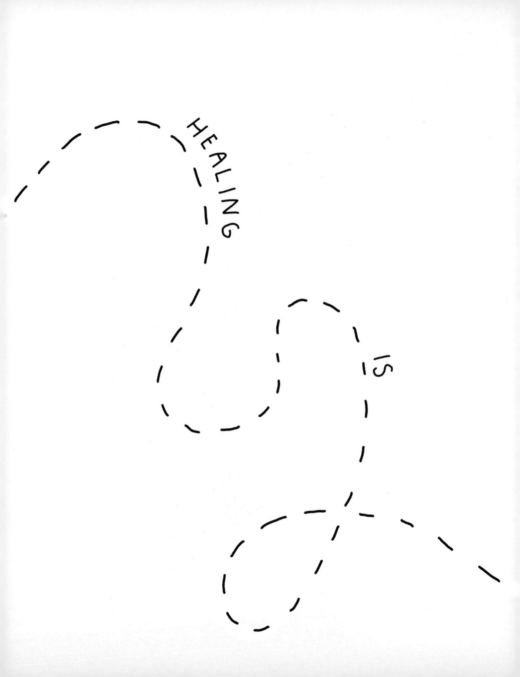

HEALING

IS

In loss we learn that we were never promised a perfect life. There are always bumps in the road . . . detours . . . unexpected pit-stops. It's a journey.

You have survived every hard thing you have gone through in your life so far.

Change is the only thing we are guaranteed in life.

Change is inevitable.
Grief is inescapable.
Loss is unavoidable.
Growth is a choice.
Insight is an intention.

I am grateful for the special people
in my life.

 I appreciate the time I have with
loved ones.

 I am thankful for the lessons and
love that come into my life.

Lean into change
rather than fighting against it.

You are capable of handling far more
than you give yourself credit for.
You are stronger than you think.

PAST

Ruminating on the past too much may foster regrets and sadness.

PRESENT

Be here in the present; it is a place you can become grounded, centred and calm.

Worrying about the future may leave you feeling anxious and stressed.

FUTURE

I can learn
to sit with
discomfort
and embrace
my emotions.

Everything doesn't 'happen for a reason'; sometimes hard and terrible things happen for no reason at all. You didn't deserve it. It wasn't your fault.

In the thick of things it may feel
like you are lost . . . remember,
there is always a way through,
even if you cannot see it yet.

'My worry can't change the future.
My regrets can't change the past.'

Your resilience is bigger than your trauma.

You will find peace . . .
not in having control,
but in surrendering it.

You are strong enough to ask
for help when you need it.

Loss is loss,
grief is grief,
no matter what form.

Sometimes it
takes loss to realise
the value of life and
what we have.

Grief is your invitation to deeply feel your emotions. To allow yourself just to be, without pretending that everything is okay . . .

... Grief invites you to turn inwards, to reflect, to put yourself and your healing first.

Nothing is forever.

First published in 2022

Text and Illustrations Copyright ©Rebekah Ballagh, 2022

Allen & Unwin
Level 2, 10 College Hill
Auckland 1011, New Zealand
Phone: (64 9) 377 3800

Email: info@allenandunwin.com
Web: www.allenandunwin.co.nz

83 Alexander Street
Crows Nest NSW 2065, Australia
Phone: (61 2) 8425 0100

A catalogue record for this book is available
from the National Library of New Zealand

ISBN 978 1 98854 786 2

Design by Kate Barraclough
Printed and bound in China by C&C Printing Co Ltd

10 9 8 7 6 5 4 3 2 1